KIRKWOOD

A Walk through History

KATHY SCHRENK

REEDY PRESS

DEDICATION

For my family: Nathan, Arthur, Noah, and Helen;
with thanks to all the people of Kirkwood, who make it a great place for us to live.

Copyright © 2022. Reedy Press, LLC
All rights reserved.

Reedy Press
PO Box 5131
St. Louis, MO 63139
www.reedypress.com

Design: Richard Roden

Cover image: This image is in the public domain,
Creative Commons CC0 1.0 Universal Public Domain.
Contents image: Unknown copyright. Image obtained from
The State Historical Society of Missouri.
Unless otherwise noted, all book images are courtesy of the author
or believed to be in the public domain.

ISBN: 9781681063997

Printed in the United States

22 23 24 25 26   5 4 3 2 1

We (the publisher and the author) have done our best to provide the most accurate information available when this book was completed. However, we make no warranty, guaranty, or promise about the accuracy, completeness, or currency of the information provided, and we expressly disclaim all warranties, express or implied. Please note that attractions, company names, addresses, websites, and phone numbers are subject to change or closure, and this is outside of our control. We are not responsible for any loss, damage, injury, or inconvenience that may occur due to the use of this book. When exploring new destinations, please do your homework before you go. You are responsible for your own safety and health when using this book. Also note that some stops on this walk are currently occupied, private residences. Please be respectful and remain on the sidewalk and not on private property.

CONTENTS

DRESSING UP FOR KIRKWOOD'S CENTENNIAL, 1965
SOURCE: KIRKWOOD HISTORICAL SOCIETY

INTRODUCTION

History buffs would be hard-pressed to find a burg in St. Louis County more devoted to preserving the structures and memories of the past than Kirkwood. It's a place that is deeply rooted in and greatly values its own history. The town has lavishly celebrated each big birthday, going as far back as number 75 in 1940, with parades, fireworks, publications, and proclamations. Its centerpiece building is one of its oldest—the 1893 train station—and is even featured on the city logo.

GREEN TREE PARADE, 1974
SOURCE: KIRKWOOD HISTORICAL SOCIETY

The downtown is filled with historic buildings and public art that pay tribute to the long history of the town. Neighborhoods close to downtown and further afield are set aside as historic districts. They include the first mansions built in the blocks surrounding downtown in the 1850s and 1860s. But the historic districts also protect Craftsman bungalows built in the 1920s, as well as mid-century modern ranches constructed in the post-war era. These and the vacation cottages built in the 1890s as part of a summer resort on the Meramec River all fall under the protection of the Landmarks Commission. Dozens of buildings have been brought back from the brink of demolition.

The city's parks department gets into the act as well. Emmenegger Nature Park preserves land once owned by the infamous Lemp family as a country retreat. A historic Black cemetery was made a park in order to help restore and recover information about the many unmarked or unclearly marked graves.

Kirkwood was established in 1853 when a group of investors formed the Kirkwood Association, which bought land surrounding the Pacific Railroad in order to create a town for people who wanted to commute to St. Louis. Kirkwood residents were pioneers in a sense, putting an emphasis on getting away from the settled and over crowded city and making a life

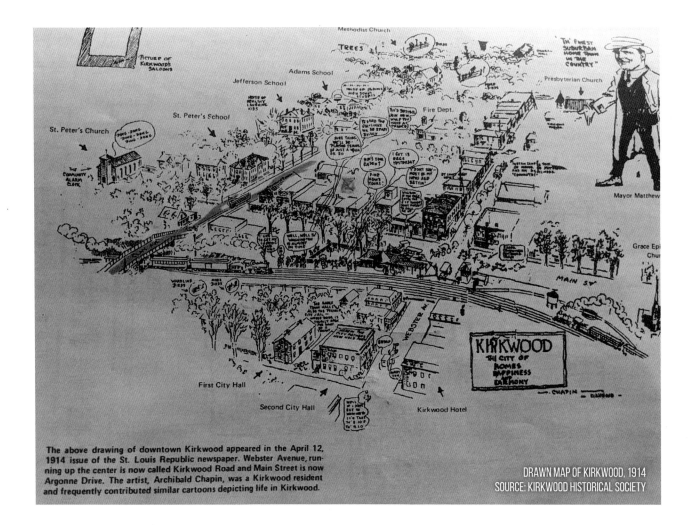

The above drawing of downtown Kirkwood appeared in the April 12, 1914 issue of the St. Louis Republic newspaper. Webster Avenue, running up the center is now called Kirkwood Road and Main Street is now Argonne Drive. The artist, Archibald Chapin, was a Kirkwood resident and frequently contributed similar cartoons depicting life in Kirkwood.

DRAWN MAP OF KIRKWOOD, 1914
SOURCE: KIRKWOOD HISTORICAL SOCIETY

in what was then little more than wilderness. In spring of 1853, the first trains arrived in Kirkwood at a precursor to the beloved train depot, having followed the route chosen by chief engineer James P. Kirkwood.

The rush west after the discovery of gold near Sacramento, California, and the power of the railroad to feed westward expansion were high on the minds of many Americans at the end of the 1840s and start of the 1850s. It would be nearly 20 years before railroad boosters struck the Golden Spike to complete the Transcontinental Railroad in Utah. So Kirkwood felt on the edge of a wilderness frontier, with hundreds of miles of mad lawlessness of uncolonized areas just to its west. It was a dry town for decades, and "proper" residents were aghast when Meramec

Highlands Resort just to the west along the resort's namesake river started serving guests booze. Kirkwoodians saw their city on a hill as a place removed, appropriate for big families, as do many residents today.

The city has always been a microcosm of what's going on in the country as a whole. Pre-Civil War residents enslaved Black people, and vigorously held to the tenets of segregation until legally forced to abandon it. Its young men were conscripted into conflicts across the globe. It enjoyed the post-WWII boom times of many similar villages. And Kirkwood's numerous examples of fine homes from across the decades make it a destination for architecture lovers.

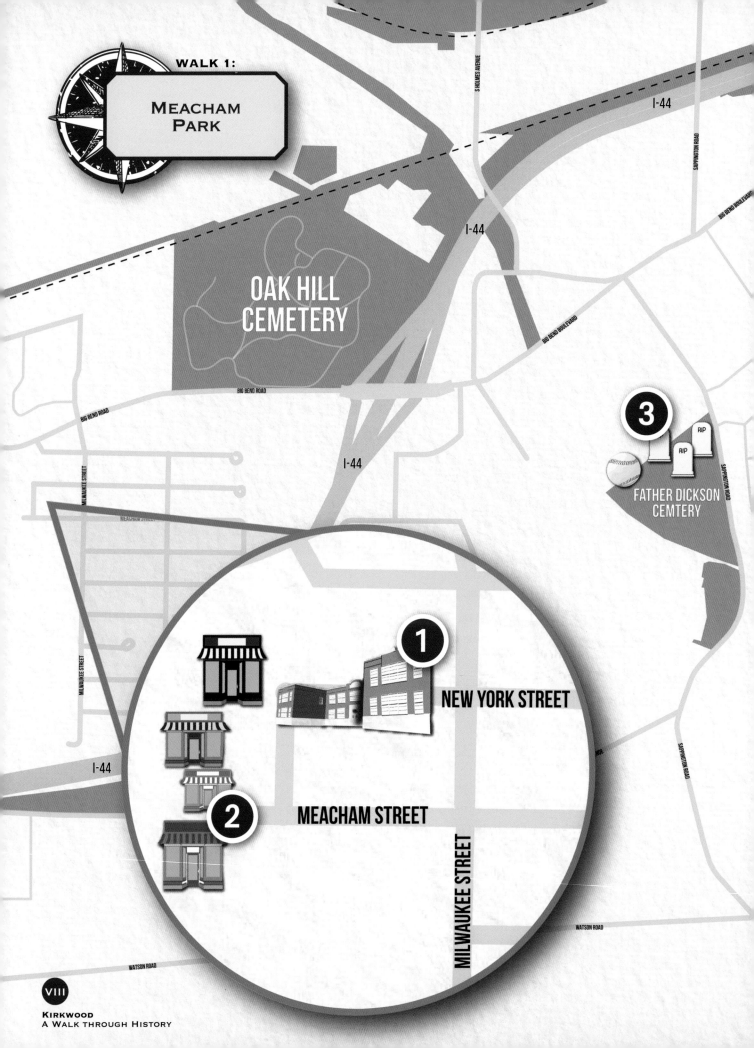

WALK 1:

MEACHAM PARK

OAK HILL CEMETERY

BIG BEND ROAD

BIG BEND ROAD

BIG BEND BOULEVARD

BIG BEND BOULEVARD

S HOLMES AVENUE

SAPPINGTON ROAD

I-44

I-44

I-44

I-44

MILWAUKEE STREET

MEACHAM STREET

MILWAUKEE STREET

③ FATHER DICKSON CEMTERY

RIP

RIP

SAPPINGTON ROAD

① NEW YORK STREET

MEACHAM STREET

②

MILWAUKEE STREET

WATSON ROAD

WATSON ROAD

SAPPINGTON ROAD

MEACHAM PARK

START AND END:
TURNER SCHOOL, MEACHAM AND MILWAUKEE STREETS
PARKING:
AMPLE STREET PARKING
WALKING TOUR DISTANCE:
ABOUT .5 MILES, OR TWO MILES IF WALKING TO FATHER DICKSON

Meacham Park is one of the most historically significant parts of Kirkwood, but may be the area that gets the least attention from historic preservationists. The neighborhood dates to the nineteenth century, just like the rest of Kirkwood. But the area didn't become part of Kirkwood until 1991, and its historic buildings were largely left to fall victim to the bulldozers of progress. Despite its importance to the Black community of the region, it has been chipped away over the decades to make room for an interstate highway and big-box retail stores that have further isolated the community.

Despite the difficulty Meacham Park has seen in preserving the physical evidence of its past, volunteers, historians, and educators have worked hard to preserve memories. It's worth a visit to understand the past and present of this area.

TURNER CLASS OF 1934
SOURCE: MEACHAM PARK FOREVER

1. TURNER SCHOOL
MEACHAM AND MILWAUKEE

The two-story brick building started as Meacham Park School in 1925. Its predecessor was a one-room house at the east end of New York Street. That school was opened in 1911 after the Black residents of the neighborhood fought for years for their own school so pupils wouldn't have to walk two miles each way to Geyer and Adams to the only school Black children were allowed to attend.

JAMES TURNER
SOURCE: KIRKWOOD
HISTORICAL SOCIETY

James Milton Turner School escaped the wrecking ball for decades and was placed on the National Register of Historic Places in 2002. Historians believe it is the last Black school remaining from before 1954, when segregation was outlawed, in St. Louis County.

The school was renamed in 1932 for Turner, who was born in 1840 to an enslaved mother. He was educated in secretly run schools in the St. Louis area, in violation of Missouri law that prohibited any education of Black people. He later became a teacher and a campaigner for Black education.

DIRECTIONS:
Walk west.

MEACHAM GROCERY
SOURCE: MEACHAM PARK FOREVER

2. OLD MEACHAM BUSINESSES
WEST OF TURNER SCHOOL, CURRENTLY LOCATION OF DEPARTMENT STORES

Just west of the school was the heart of the Meacham Park business district at the corner of

MCCULLOUGH GROCERY,
SE CORNER OF MEACHAM AND SHELBY
SOURCE: MEACHAM PARK FOREVER

Shelby and Meacham Avenues. This was where the first Black-owned store opened in 1919. D. M. Powell opened the store, which became a hub of activity for decades.

Meacham Park was founded in 1892 by Elzey Meacham, a white real estate developer from Memphis. He established other subdivisions in the south before coming to St. Louis County and registering the subdivision of Meacham Park.

In 1991, Kirkwood annexed Meacham Park. More than two-thirds of the neighborhood's residents voted in favor of the annexation, hoping the city would devote more resources

MEACHAM PARK BUSINESS DISTRICT, 1920s
SOURCE: MEACHAM PARK FOREVER

to maintaining Meacham Park's infrastructure. They got that, but they also lost hundreds of homes to the Kirkwood Commons development, which now includes Walmart and Target. The city bought some of those homes from willing sellers, and took some via eminent domain.

DIRECTIONS:

Because the construction of Interstate 44 cut through Meacham Park, there isn't a great way to walk to the cemetery. Go north on Milwaukee, then east on Big Bend and turn right on Grants Trail. Or, return to your vehicle and drive east on Big Bend Road for about a mile, then turn right on Sappington Road. Turn right just past the cemetery and park in the Grant's Trail trailhead parking lot.

3. CEMETERY AND BALL FIELD
845 SAPPINGTON ROAD

Father Dickson Cemetery is part of the Ulysses S. Grant National Historic Site. It was founded

FATHER DICKSON CEMETERY

in 1903 as one of the few Black cemeteries in the county. Turner is one of the many local luminaries buried there.

In the 1920s and 1930s, grocer D. M. Powell sponsored a winning baseball team that played teams from around the region, often at the ball field next to the cemetery. The area was known as Spring Bottoms due to the natural spring found in the area. Meacham Park folks accessed the area via a spur railroad. Today a small residential neighborhood and some industrial businesses occupy the area where the crack of the bat was once heard.

FATHER DICKSON CEMETERY

DID YOU KNOW?

Quinette Cemetery (see page 32), Father Dickson Cemetery, and others around the region and the country are seeing a surge of interest in restoring Black cemeteries. Quinette fell victim to vandalism and overgrowth over the years. Volunteers and advocates have uncovered gravestones and done extensive research to fill in the gaps in information about who was buried where, in the name of preserving Black cultural heritage and helping people trace their family lines.

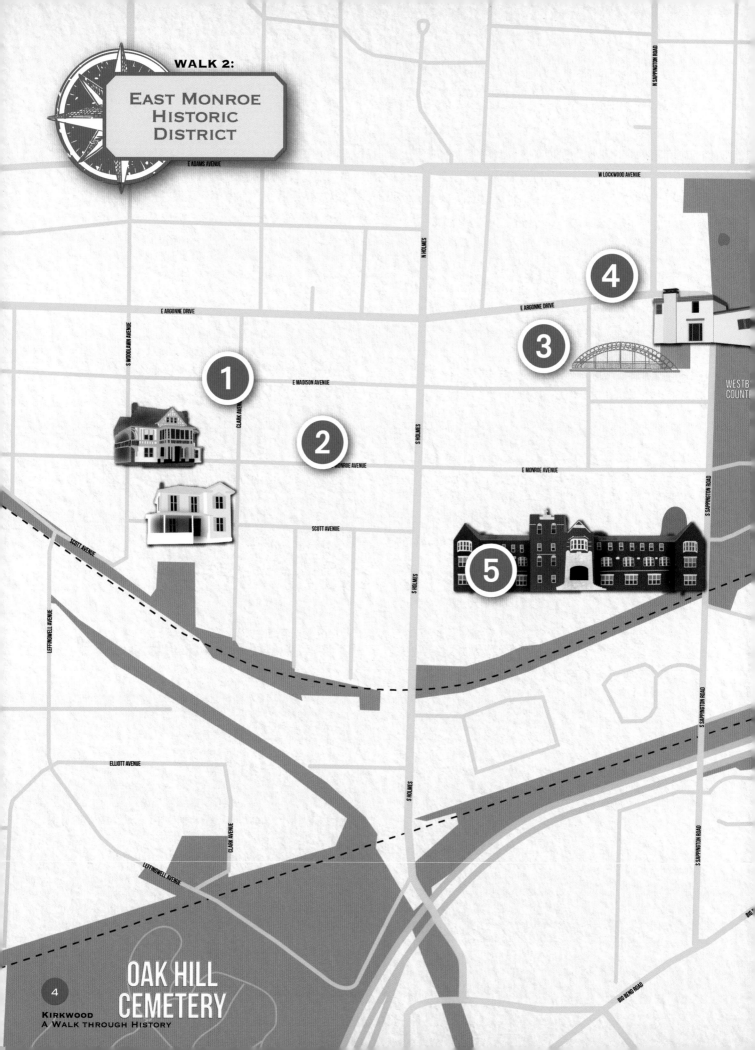

E ADAMS AVENUE

W LOCKWOOD AVENUE

N SAPPINGTON ROAD

E ARGONNE DRIVE

S WOODLAWN AVENUE

N HOLMES

4

3

E ARGONNE DRIVE

WESTB COUNTI

1

E MADISON AVENUE

CLARK AVENUE

S HOLMES

2

MONROE AVENUE

E MONROE AVENUE

S SAPPINGTON ROAD

SCOTT AVENUE

SCOTT AVENUE

LEFFINGWELL AVENUE

5

S HOLMES

ELLIOTT AVENUE

CLARK AVENUE

S SAPPINGTON ROAD

S SAPPINGTON ROAD

LEFFINGWELL AVENUE

BIG BEND ROAD

BIG

OAK HILL CEMETERY

EAST MONROE HISTORIC DISTRICT

SAPPINGTON-AREA MID-CENTURY MODERN HOMES

START AND END:
MONROE AND WOODLAWN AVENUES
PARKING:
AMPLE STREET PARKING
WALKING TOUR DISTANCE:
ABOUT 2 MILES

There are two distinct sections of this walk, and while they are close together geographically, they could hardly be farther apart in their architectural styles. The first has much in common with the Victorian, Italianate, and Greek Revival styles in the nearby Jefferson-Argonne and North Taylor historic districts. It also is home to a favorite of the folks from the 1904 World's Fair Society, an active group of history buffs who continue to commemorate that event well into the 21st century.

The second section of this walk is through a neighborhood that has more in common with mid-century districts one would find in a West Coast suburb, or with the aesthetic of the Frank Lloyd Wright house on the west side of Kirkwood. The neighborhood also includes the 100-year-old majestic brick building that's home to a beloved Catholic girls' academy.

SEVEN GABLES

 **1. MONROE: SEVEN GABLES**
MONROE AND WOODLAWN

On the northeast corner of the Monroe-Woodlawn intersection is the house known as Seven Gables, or the Judge Enos Clarke house. The Tudor Revival home was built in 1913 and is individually registered on the National Register of Historic Places.

Across Woodlawn Avenue is the Sutherland Mitchell Shallcross house, built in 1862.

Home over the years to three Missouri state representatives, it's a large Victorian considered "highly intact." Its wide wrap-around porch—restored in the 2000s after being removed in the 1940s—and overall aesthetic seem to embrace its status as one of the oldest houses in Kirkwood.

DIRECTIONS:
Walk west on Monroe and turn left on Smith Street, then left on Scott Avenue. Check out the World's Fair house, and then continue on Scott. Turn left on Woodlawn and make another right to continue on Scott. After viewing the homes on that block, return to Monroe via either Clark or Holmes.

2. MONROE HISTORIC DISTRICT
BETWEEN SMITH AND HOLMES

The World's Fair Wisconsin House is at 415 Scott Avenue. The Tudor Revival was built in 1904 on the grounds of the World's Fair in Forest Park and was disassembled and moved to this location in 1905. The house was altered somewhat when it was rebuilt but maintains the chalet-style it had when it hosted visitors in Forest Park. (The Nevada and West Virginia houses are in nearby Oakland.)

The block of Scott Avenue bounded by Woodlawn, Clark, and the railroad tracks is home to the Grissom-Ewing House, one of the largest houses of its age in the area and a local landmark. It's also home to the Hazard house, an Italianate home built in 1870, which was awarded a "maintenance of merit" award by the Kirkwood Landmarks Commission in 2009 for its "splendid" roof replacement.

The Unsell house, built in 1873 on the 600 block of East Monroe, is another highly intact Italianate house on the National Register.

1862 HOUSE ON WOODLAWN

DIRECTIONS:
Walk east on Monroe one block and turn left on Brent Avenue. Then turn right on Westwood Place and left on Minturn Avenue.

MINTURN PARK

3. MINTURN PARK
MINTURN AND ARGONNE

This part of the walk leaves Kirkwood proper for Oakland, a tiny municipality just to the east. The first stop is Minturn Park, a small but scenic green space set amongst Ursuline Academy, the Kirkwood School District's Early Child Center, and Westborough Country Club. A picturesque pedestrian bridge spans Gravois

Creek that runs through the park and the neighborhood. The bridge was designed by local architect and former Oakland Mayor Paul Marti. The park also has a rain garden and a pollinator garden, and is surrounded by some of the most interesting modern homes in the area.

DIRECTIONS:

Walk north from Minturn Park to Argonne Drive and turn right. Continue to the right as Argonne ends and you find yourself on Sappington Road. After viewing the Topsy Turvy House, continue to Singlepath Lane.

4. BOHEMIAN ENCLAVE
SAPPINGTON ROAD BETWEEN MONROE AND ARGONNE

It's hard to miss the home on the 100 block of South Sappington Road known as the Topsy Turvy House. The white stucco building features a room on its north side that is built at an angle to the rest of the house. A small berm and landscape feature mimic the angle of the room and give the viewer the impression of being at one of those roadside attraction vortices where gravity and physics seem out of whack.

This neighborhood was known as home to professors, LGBTQ people, and other followers of a "Bohemian" lifestyle. In the post-war

TOPSY TURVY HOUSE IN BOHEMIAN ENCLAVE

DID YOU KNOW?

Harris Armstrong was one of finalists in the design competition for the Gateway Arch. He designed many local landmarks, including the Ethical Society building on Clayton Road.

decades, rumors sometimes flew in the surrounding neighborhoods about the debauchery of the people living in this new house style, which is now so highly regarded.

Continuing on Singlepath Lane, the once home and studio of famed architect Harris Armstrong looks out on the gardens and the country club. The effect is a melding of indoor and outdoor, in the tradition of Frank Lloyd Wright. The gardens feature a species of conifer rare to the Midwest: the Chinese Larch, which has the unusual characteristic of its needles changing color in the fall. It was brought to the area for exhibit in the 1904 World's Fair and some samples remained in the area after.

CHINESE LARCH IN BOHEMIAN ENCLAVE

DIRECTIONS:
Walk south on Sappington to the corner of Monroe to see the Ursuline property.

5. URSULINE ACADEMY
341 SAPPINGTON ROAD

Catholic nuns known as the Ursuline Sisters founded the first St. Louis academy in 1848 on Fifth Street in downtown St. Louis. The women were immigrants from central Europe who opened the school less than two months after arriving in St. Louis. Two years later, they built a new school at 12th and Russell streets, where St. Joseph's Croatian Church now stands.

After 25 years, the academy needed even more space and bought the 28-acre property in Oakland at the corner of Sappington and Monroe. A mansion on the grounds served as the school building for about 10 years. The school moved in to the brick building that is still the backbone of the campus in 1926.

URSULINE ACADEMY, CIRCA 1940
SOURCE: SOURCE: THE STATE HISTORICAL SOCIETY OF MISSOURI

URSULINE ACADEMY CAMPUS

FRANK LLOYD WRIGHT HOME IN KIRKWOOD
SOURCE: MARY STRIEGEL, WIKIMEDIA COMMONS

DID YOU KNOW?

One of only five Frank Lloyd Wright houses in Missouri is in Kirkwood, on the west side of town. The house was designed and built in the 1950s. The house-museum is on 10 acres known as Ebsworth Park and is available for tours.

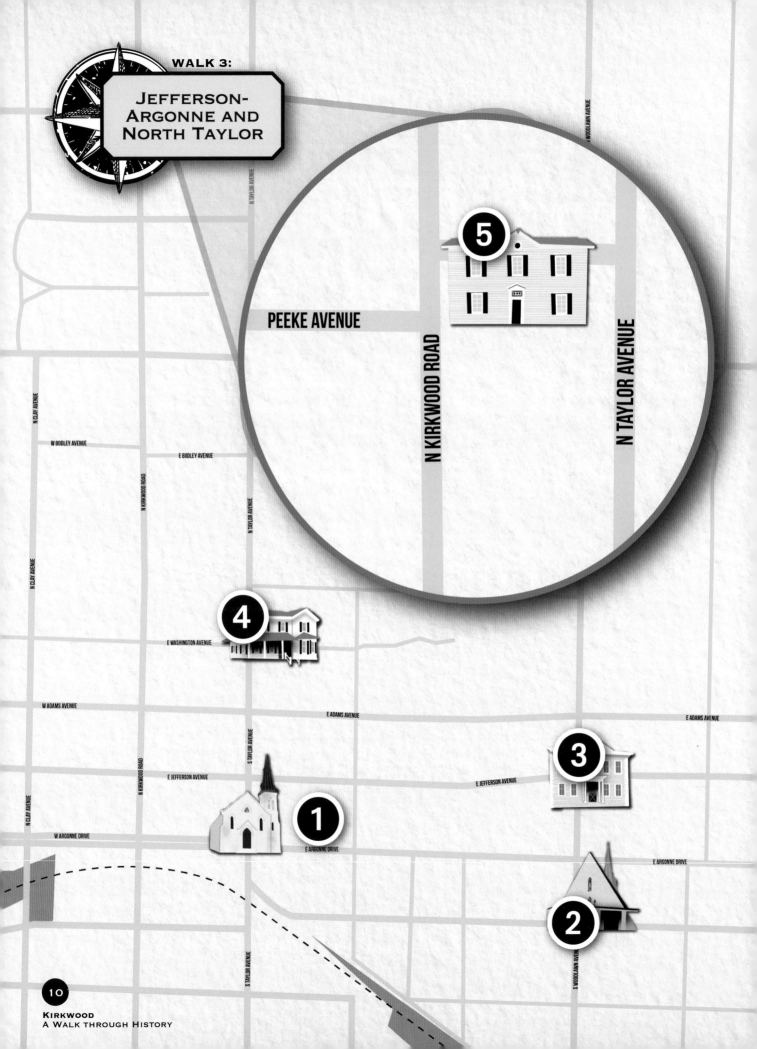

PEEKE AVENUE

N KIRKWOOD ROAD

N TAYLOR AVENUE

S WOODLAWN AVENUE

N TAYLOR AVENUE

5

N CLAY AVENUE

W BODLEY AVENUE

E BODLEY AVENUE

N KIRKWOOD ROAD

N TAYLOR AVENUE

N CLAY AVENUE

4

E WASHINGTON AVENUE

W ADAMS AVENUE

E ADAMS AVENUE

E ADAMS AVENUE

S TAYLOR AVENUE

3

E JEFFERSON AVENUE

N KIRKWOOD ROAD

E JEFFERSON AVENUE

E JEFFERSON AVENUE

N CLAY AVENUE

1

W ARGONNE DRIVE

E ARGONNE DRIVE

E ARGONNE DRIVE

2

S WOODLAWN AVENUE

S TAYLOR AVENUE

JEFFERSON-ARGONNE AND NORTH TAYLOR HISTORIC DISTRICTS

START AND END:
ARGONNE DRIVE AT TAYLOR AVENUE
PARKING:
AMPLE STREET PARKING
WALKING TOUR DISTANCE:
3 MILES

Much like today, in the second half of the nineteenth century the wealthy of St. Louis looked to Kirkwood for quieter streets and larger home lots on which to raise families. The areas northeast and east of the train station were a particular draw, with large houses and vast estates suited to very large families. The Byars house, for instance, in the 400 block of North Taylor, housed 14 children. "I love children," William Byars wrote in a letter to his mother. "I don't care how many we have, just so I can feed them." Byars made his living writing for the *Post-Dispatch*, *Globe Democrat*, and *New York Journal*, as well as pamphlets and articles he published himself. The historic record is silent on how he fed 14 children working as a writer.

ELIOT CHAPEL DETAIL

1. ARGONNE DRIVE
BETWEEN TAYLOR AND CLARK

Start this walk at the corner of Argonne Drive and Taylor Avenue. The intersection is dominated by Eliot Unitarian Chapel, one of the oldest church buildings in Kirkwood. The English Gothic Revival building was built by Grace Episcopal Church in 1859 and is listed on the National Register of Historic

GRACE EPISCOPAL CHURCH
SOURCE: LIBRARY OF CONGRESS

GILL HOUSE

owner chronicled the dramatic renovation of the 1858 mansion after it had fallen into disrepair; it had been named an "endangered residence" in 2009 by the Kirkwood Landmarks Commission.

Places. The original building featured a square tower and steeple towering 83 feet above the street. It was designed by Robert S. Mitchell, also the architect of the Old Courthouse in downtown St. Louis.

GRACE CHURCH DEDICATION, 1960
SOURCE: GRACE CHURCH

Walking east down Argonne takes you into the Jefferson-Argonne Historic District, featuring some of the oldest houses in town. Many proudly display signs on their property announcing their homes' date of construction. Italianate and Victorian styles dominate the 19th century construction and many homeowners highlight this feature by painting decorative trim in contrasting colors. The Gill House at 419 E. Argonne Street garnered more than 30,000 Instagram followers when the

HISTORY HOUSE
SOURCE: KIRKWOOD HISTORICAL SOCIETY

Also known as the History House, the McLaglan-Black House at 549 E. Argonne Street was home to the Kirkwood Historical Society from 1972-1992. (The society is now at Mudd's Grove on West Argonne; see page 25.)

(The society is now at Mudd's Grove on West Argonne; see page 25.)

DID YOU KNOW?

The Jefferson-Argonne Historic District was recognized in 2007 and the North Taylor district in 2011. The Jefferson-Argonne district has six houses individually listed on the National Register of Historic Places, while the North Taylor district has one.

HISTORY HOUSE DETAIL

It is one of the more dramatically beautiful Italianate-style houses in the district, with a three-story square tower capping the 1863 home.

DIRECTIONS:
Cross to the south side of Argonne.

2. GRACE CHURCH
514 E. ARGONNE DRIVE

Grace Episcopal Church was one of the first places of worship established in the budding town of Kirkwood. It started unofficially

GRACE CHURCH

in the parlor of Harry Bodley's home in 1853. Neighbors and fellow participants in the readings included some of the town fathers whose names are known to this day, such as Hiram Leffingwell.

The original Grace Church, now Eliot Chapel, was built in 1859. This much larger building was constructed in 1960.

DIRECTIONS:
Turn around at Clark Avenue (the east edge of the Grace Church property) and then turn right onto Woodlawn.

3. WOODLAWN AND JEFFERSON AVENUES
JEFFERSON AVENUE BETWEEN WOODLAWN AND FILLMORE

This neighborhood (extending east to Holmes Avenue just as the town boundary does) is

GREENSFELDER HOUSE, WOODLAWN
SOURCE: KIRKWOOD HISTORICAL SOCIETY

home to some of the first streets laid out when the city was incorporated. In those days the lots were one to nearly two-and-a-half acres. In the decades since, Kirkwood has allowed most of those to be subdivided, so now there are lots as small as 15,000 feet. The neighborhood's homes were built before 1900 for families wanting vast estates in this planned suburb, as well as bungalows built in the 1920s and 1930s as part of tract projects.

One of the oldest houses in the city is on Woodlawn as you walk north from Argonne to Jefferson. The Keith-Greensfelder House was built in 1850 for David Keith, one of the founders of First Presbyterian Church.

A block to the west at Jefferson and Fillmore is one of the oldest standing houses

SMITH-KEYSOR HOUSE

in Kirkwood: the Smith-Keysor House, built in 1853. It was purchased from the original owner, Spencer Smith, in 1912, by William Keysor, who was a professor of law at Washington University. He was also president of the Kirkwood school board, and the elementary school on Geyer Road was named after him. It's listed on the National Register of Historic Places, along with a house across the intersection at 235 E. Jefferson Street.

In 2004, the Historical Society estimated that fewer than 10 new homes in the Jefferson-Argonne neighborhood had been constructed since 1950, out of 146 properties.

DIRECTIONS:
Walk west for one block and turn right (north) on Taylor Avenue. Turn left and walk half a block to view the Halsey-Rode house, next to the modern YMCA building. Then return to Taylor. Pass Walker Park to enter the North Taylor Historic District.

4. TAYLOR HISTORIC DISTRICT BETWEEN JEFFERSON AND BODLEY
TAYLOR AVENUE BETWEEN JEFFERSON AND BODLEY

The North Taylor Avenue Historic District is newer than the Jefferson-Argonne designation but is no less significant or picturesque. In their application to the Department of the Interior for inclusion in the National Register of Historic Places, city officials called the area "a tour through architectural time." It provides evidence of the early-nineteenth-century agricultural nature of the area, the privileged and idealistic attitudes of the early commuter culture in the second half of the nineteenth century, and the democratization of the area after the city was incorporated.

Known as the Halsey-Rode House, this cottage may be humble but has been important to the city residents since it was built in 1860. It

HALSEY-RODE HOUSE

was constructed by Egbert Halsey, the architect of Kirkwood's first permanent school building. And it has been used by the YMCA and other civic organizations as a gathering place. The 400 block of North Taylor includes the 1883 Orrick House, considered one of the area's top examples of a renovated home that retained its original charm. The block also is home to the

BYARS HOUSE
SOURCE: KIRKWOOD HISTORICAL SOCIETY

Byars House, which was part of a 153-acre land grant acquired by the Holmes Family in 1830. Finally, the farmhouse Victorian-style Essex-Gamble House, built in 1865, is on this block as well.

5. TAYLOR HISTORIC DISTRICT NORTH OF BODLEY
TAYLOR AVENUE BETWEEN BODLEY AND SWAN

The Beckstein-Ashley home on the 700 block of north Kirkwood Road goes all the way back to the very earliest days of Kirkwood settlement. It was built in 1860 but the lot is also the site of the graves of three children who died in the 1840s and 1850s. The gravestones are stored out of sight on the property.

As you return to Taylor and walk north, you will see homes mostly built in the 1920s and 1930s in Dutch Colonial, Colonial, Tudor, Queen Anne, and Victorian styles. The closer the tour gets to Manchester Road, the more houses you'll see built in the 1920s and late 1940s—before the Great Depression and after World War II.

The 700 and 800 blocks of North Taylor include newer homes interspersed with ones built in the 1850s and 1860s, including examples of Greek Revival and Victorian Italianate.

The home at 549 N. Taylor is the only one in the North Taylor district individually listed on the National Register of Historic Places. It earned this designation because of the integrity of its Craftsman design. It has been well-maintained since it was built in 1922 and signifies the affluence and optimism of those who settled in Kirkwood in its early decades.

DID YOU KNOW?

The architectural style known as "Italianate" is inspired by southern European buildings but is actually American. Common characteristics of this style include tall, slim windows; a central, square cupola; and deep eaves supported by decorative brackets.

WALK 4:

DOWNTOWN

E JEFFERSON AVENUE

N TAYLOR AVENUE

N KIRKWOOD ROAD

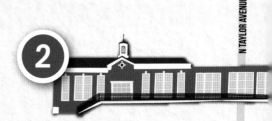

②

W ARGONNE DRIVE

④

W ARGONNE DRIVE

E ARGONNE DRIVE

E ARGONNE DRIVE

①

S TAYLOR AVENUE

③

⑤

McEntee Park

S KIRKWOOD ROAD

W MADISON AVENUE

W MADISON AVENUE

⑥

S TAYLOR AVENUE

E MONROE AVENUE

E MONROE AVENUE

S KIRKWOOD ROAD

DOWNTOWN

START AND END:
ARGONNE DRIVE AT TAYLOR AVENUE
PARKING:
AMPLE STREET PARKING
WALKING TOUR DISTANCE:
APPROXIMATELY .75 MILES

Downtown Kirkwood is a tremendous source of pride for the leadership and residents of the town. Popular restaurants—some comforting classics that have been in place for decades, and others new and trendy—and vibrant retail storefronts—selling wares from vegetable seeds to giftable sweets to high-end clothes and jewelry—blanket the downtown historic district. The retail area, which includes plenty of modern residential-above-retail buildings several stories high, extends a block in each direction from Kirkwood Road and from Bodley Avenue and south nearly to Woodbine Avenue and the famous Magic House.

This tour doesn't stray far from the center of downtown, which is found at the intersection of Argonne Drive and Kirkwood Road (known as Lindbergh Road outside of Kirkwood). Still, there is much to see in an area of only a few blocks.

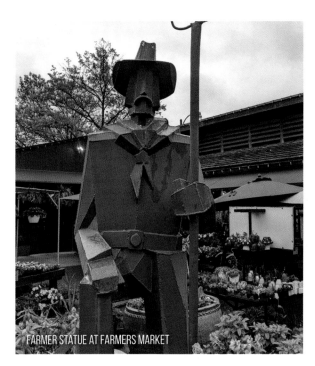

FARMER STATUE AT FARMERS MARKET

 1. FARMERS MARKET AND PUBLIC ART
ARGONNE DRIVE BETWEEN KIRKWOOD AND TAYLOR

The Kirkwood Farmers Market is a hub of activity nearly year-round with summer produce, fall pumpkins, and holiday-season tree sales. Kirkwood created the market as a Centennial project in 1976. Before that, the corner of Argonne and Taylor was home to the

3 STACKED CHAIRS

2. KIRKWOOD LIBRARY
140 E. JEFFERSON AVENUE

The stately brick building that houses the library (deemed "Missouri Library of the Year" in 2007) at Jefferson and Taylor Avenues was built in 1940. Prior to that it was housed on the second floor of City Hall after the League of Women Voters made it a priority for their organization in 1922. It was the first tax-supported library in St. Louis County.

The building was expanded in the mid-1950s and again in the mid-1960s. It was remodeled in 2009. Ten years later, the cupola on the building was removed and restored before being put back in to place.

DIRECTIONS:
Return south to Argonne Drive via Taylor. Turn right (west) and cross Kirkwood Road to get to the train station.

railroad siding where freight trains would pull aside to allow faster trains to pass.

In the center of Argonne Drive on this block is one of Kirkwood's best-known pieces of public art, *3 Stacked Chairs*, by local artist Mel Meyer. Meyer also created the green metal sculpture of a farmer watching over the block, as well as other modern sculptures in town.

DIRECTIONS:
Walk north on Taylor Avenue one block to reach the library.

KIRKWOOD LIBRARY

KIRKWOOD LIBRARY, CIRCA 1945
SOURCE: THE STATE HISTORICAL SOCIETY OF MISSOURI

DID YOU KNOW?

The Kirkwood Arts Commission was founded in 2014 to bring more public art to the city, continuing the previous efforts of the Kirkwood Area Arts Council. Modern sculptures curated by the city are found in downtown Kirkwood, at Kirkwood Park, at Walker Park, and on the Meramec College campus.

KIRKWOOD TRAIN STATION

KIRKWOOD TRAIN STATION, CIRCA 1951
SOURCE: THE STATE HISTORICAL SOCIETY OF MISSOURI

 ## 3. TRAIN STATION
110 W. ARGONNE DRIVE

The train station might be the most beloved building in Kirkwood. It's even on the city logo. Of course, the city owes its very existence to the railroad. Kirkwood is often referred to as the first planned suburb west of the Mississippi, and the town was placed where it was because of the path of the railroad.

The building continues to be a working train station, serving passengers who ride the Missouri River Runner between St. Louis and Kansas City. In 2002, Amtrak threatened to close the station due to budget issues. But so many volunteers rallied to help that the city bought it and it has operated without interruption, despite budget- and pandemic-related Amtrak service cuts.

The first depot was built in 1853, the same year the Kirkwood Association bought the land that would become Kirkwood. The existing station with the distinctive conical roof over the bay facing the tracks was erected in 1893. It was placed on the National Register of Historic Places in 1985 in recognition of its historical significance and Romanesque architecture.

DIRECTIONS:
Cross Argonne Drive.

 ## 4. FEED STORE, FIRE HOUSE AND OLD POST OFFICE
100 BLOCK OF W. ARGONNE DRIVE

This block of Argonne Drive is packed full of historic buildings, most of which now house trendy retail establishments and restaurants. First is the Coulter Feed Store Building,

COULTER FEED BUILDING

COULTER FEED BUILDING, CIRCA 1950
SOURCE: THE STATE HISTORICAL SOCIETY OF MISSOURI

DID YOU KNOW?

A train turntable was located near the present-day farmers market to turn engines for the return trip to St. Louis. It also housed "helper engines" for getting freight trains up the hill to the Kirkwood station. Commuter trains traveled through Kirkwood until 1961.

built in 1912. It's a highly visible landmark, perhaps second only to the train station for its recognizability.

A few doors west is the 1920 firehouse, one of a very few mission-style buildings in Kirkwood. Next to that is the 1932 Old Post Office, a neoclassical building often painted with its trim contrasting the main color for a striking visual effect.

Most of these buildings are replacements for structures that were lost in various fires throughout the late nineteenth and early twentieth centuries.

....

DIRECTIONS:
Walk left (south) onto Clay from Argonne. Cross the railroad tracks via the Clay Avenue overpass. Turn left on Madison Avenue and left again to access Veterans Memorial Walkway.

....

5. MEMORIAL WALKWAY AND CITY HALL
MADISON AND KIRKWOOD

This charming park space is an opportunity for a lovely walk as well as a somber reminder of tragedies in Kirkwood history. Bill McEntee

MEMORIAL WALK

Memorial Park is named for an officer who was killed in the line of duty in 2005. Continue walking north and east along the railroad tracks and view the plaques with names of those killed in a 2008 shooting during a City Council meeting that resulted in seven deaths, including that of the perpetrator.

Further along the path is another sculpture by Mel Meyer titled *Themes of Kirkwood*. Continue on toward City Hall, which was built in 1942. The nearby space for veterans' monuments was set aside in 1965.

....

DIRECTIONS:
Walk west on Madison Avenue less than a block to the Peter Bopp home. Walk right (south) onto Clay to get to Monroe Avenue, then around the block to the Henry Bopp home.

....

6. BOPP HOUSES
100 BLOCK OF W. MONROE AVENUE AND 100 BLOCK OF W. MADISON AVENUE

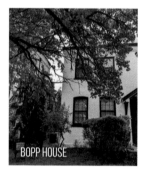

BOPP HOUSE

The Bopp name is known around the area, with a road and other businesses sharing the name. Peter Bopp Sr. was a shoemaker who moved to Kirkwood with his three sons in 1865. The family helped found the Concordia Lutheran Church on Madison Avenue and the four Bopps worked together to help build the first Concordia Chapel.

Brothers Peter Jr. and Henry Bopp built houses four years and less than a block apart. Henry's on Monroe Avenue was built in the Country Classic style and originally brick. Henry was the oldest Bopp brother and built his house in 1866. Peter Jr.'s home was a Victorian and was built in 1870.

100 BLOCK OF WEST ARGONNE, APPROX. 1900
SOURCE: KIRKWOOD HISTORICAL SOCIETY

DID YOU KNOW?

Argonne was originally Main Street, and was changed in 1919 in honor of local soldiers who fought in the Battle of Argonne Forest in World War I.

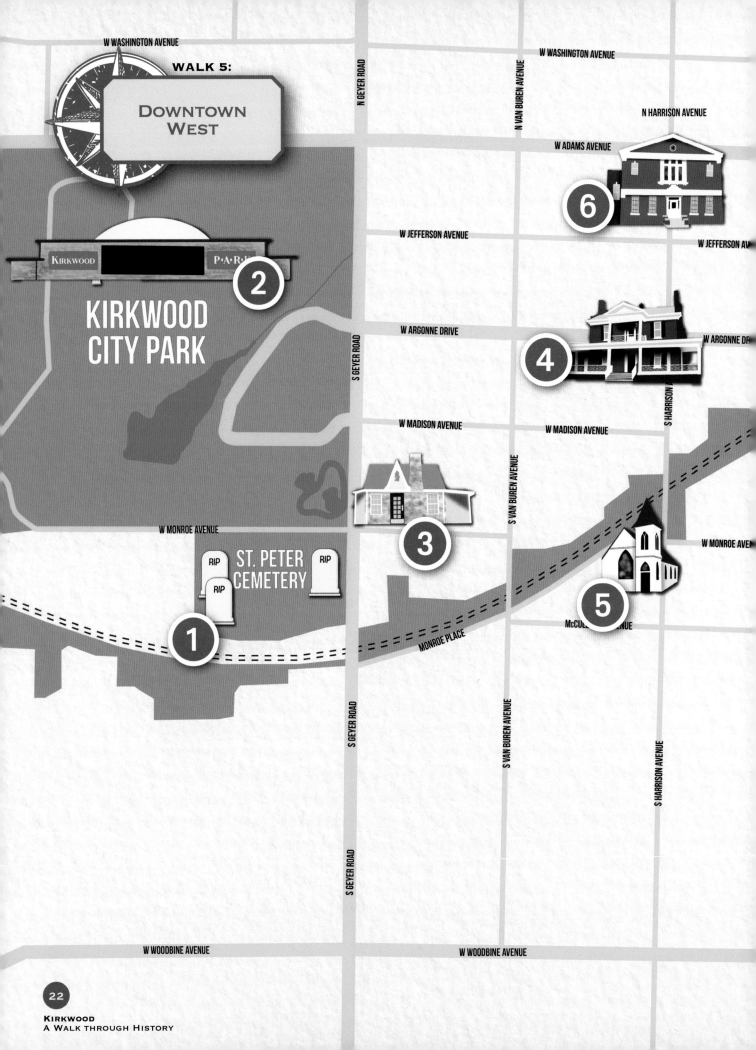

WALK 5:

DOWNTOWN WEST

W WASHINGTON AVENUE

W WASHINGTON AVENUE

N GEYER ROAD

N VAN BUREN AVENUE

N HARRISON AVENUE

W ADAMS AVENUE

6

KIRKWOOD **P·A·R·K**

2

KIRKWOOD CITY PARK

W JEFFERSON AVENUE

W JEFFERSON AV

W ARGONNE DRIVE

4

W ARGONNE DR

S GEYER ROAD

W MADISON AVENUE

W MADISON AVENUE

S VAN BUREN AVENUE

S HARRISON

3

W MONROE AVENUE

RIP ST. PETER RIP
CEMETERY

RIP

RIP

W MONROE AVE

5

McCUL...   NUE

1

MONROE PLACE

S GEYER ROAD

S VAN BUREN AVENUE

S HARRISON AVENUE

W WOODBINE AVENUE

W WOODBINE AVENUE

DOWNTOWN WEST

START AND END:
ST. PETER CEMETERY

PARKING:
ON GEYER ROAD OR IN KIRKWOOD PARK

WALKING TOUR DISTANCE:
APPROXIMATELY 1.75 MILES

ST. PETER CEMETERY

This part of Kirkwood is a potpourri of sites: the town's oldest cemetery, a historic tavern, its history museum, plus several historic homes.

West of downtown, Kirkwood becomes somewhat hillier and there are sections that can even be thought of as rural—or what passes for rural east of I-270. Kirkwood Park is a beautiful oasis with a fishing lake, trails, fields, and wooded picnic areas. Sugar Creek Valley is a neighborhood with its own identity, with large wooded lots, some that back up to Ebsworth Park, where Kirkwood's Frank Lloyd Wright home resides. Its Sugar Creek Ranch Historic District features 60 mid-century homes by Ralph and Mary Jane Fournier, an influential force in post-war home design.

1. ST. PETER CEMETERY
520 W. MONROE AVENUE

It's coming up on 190 years since this plot of land north of what would soon be the railroad, and in later years south of Kirkwood's major public park, became a cemetery. In 1835, a woman named Unity Breen became the first person buried here at the age of 28. This lot was also the site of the first St. Peter Church. It's the oldest Catholic cemetery in St. Louis County and is still active today. Many of those buried here are St. Peter priests and Ursuline nuns. The cemetery is open to the public.

The original St. Peter Church was on this site but burned down in 1875. The church was then rebuilt on its current site about half a mile away on Argonne Drive.

DIRECTIONS:
Cross Monroe Avenue.

2. KIRKWOOD PARK
GEYER ROAD BETWEEN ADAMS AND MONROE

Kirkwood's oldest park was established in 1941 with two 20-acre areas and has since grown to 92 acres. It's home to the Aquatic Center with its slides and waterplay features, the skating rink, walking paths, and even fishing in Walker Lake. There's also a community garden and plenty of places to stroll. There are even unpaved hiking trails.

KIRKWOOD PARK

Each fall the park is full of festival-goers with the city's Greentree Festival. It's perhaps the biggest event of the year in Kirkwood with more than 100 arts and crafts booths, live music, and a Folklife Festival where folks in period garb show how people worked, made tools, and played games in the 1700s and 1800s.

DIRECTIONS:
Cross Geyer Road.

3. GEYER INN
220 S. GEYER ROAD

The Geyer Inn is the kind of place where regular patrons bring their dogs and local residents might recognize their mechanic hanging out after their shift or their neighbor the accountant.

This building started out as a gas station in 1904 and was converted into a tavern in the 1930s. It had a long life as a watering hole until the long-time owner Frank Rodman passed away in 2010. The place was temporarily out of business and almost was consigned to the dust bin of history when former Blues player Jim Campbell bought the building in 2012, then reopened the tavern.

GEYER INN, VINTAGE
SOURCE: GEYER INN

GEYER INN INTERIOR

Going into its second century as a homey local drinking establishment, it continues to be a laid-back place for folks to gather.

DIRECTIONS:
Walk north one block, turn right on Argonne, and walk two blocks to the Kirkwood Historical Society.

4. MUDD'S GROVE
302 W. ARGONNE DRIVE

This stately red brick house has been home to the Kirkwood Historical Society since 1992. The society's library houses a wealth of information, including just about every school yearbook published in a Kirkwood school,

MUDD'S GROVE INTERIOR
SOURCE: LIBRARY OF CONGRESS

MUDD'S GROVE
SOURCE: KIRKWOOD HISTORICAL SOCIETY

back issues of magazines and newsletters, and binders filled with detailed information on each home in each historic district in the city. The Historical Society was founded in 1961. The house itself was built in 1859 and purchased by state legislator Henry Mudd in 1866. Mudd helped draft the Missouri state constitution and held a number of influential posts in early Missouri, including curator of the University of Missouri, and president of the Missouri State Horticulture Society.

DID YOU KNOW?

Kirkwood has nine local historic districts and four nationally recognized historic districts. It also has 85 locally registered individual buildings and 24 on the national register.

DIRECTIONS:
Walk south on Harrison for two blocks to Olive Chapel.

OLIVE CHAPEL, CIRCA 1976
SOURCE: THE STATE HISTORICAL SOCIETY OF MISSOURI

 ## 5. OLIVE CHAPEL
311 S. HARRISON AVENUE

In 1853, Olive Chapel was the second church founded in Kirkwood. It is located at 330 W. Washington Street in a stone building that also served as the first public school for Black students in the mid-19th century. In 1923, the congregation moved to the former Friedens Evangelical Lutheran church, which was built in 1896, at Monroe and Harrison Avenues.

In its earliest days, the church was served by circuit riders, or "saddlebag preachers," who rode from church to church on the frontier as itinerants to other African Methodist Episcopal (A.M.E.) churches that didn't have their own dedicated preacher. They traveled from as far east as Carondolet in St. Louis City to the Missouri River bottoms in Franklin County, near Washington, Missouri.

DIRECTIONS:
Walk north on Harrison Avenue for three blocks.

6. NORTH HARRISON AVENUE
HARRISON BETWEEN JEFFERSON AND WAY

These blocks of Harrison include several historic buildings. The Masonic Lodge at 211 N. Harrison Avenue was originally the C. D. Ricker home. The Masons bought, remodeled, and dedicated it in 1921. They had started meeting in a nearby building in 1873, and members included some of the founders of Kirkwood.

The Swan Cottage on the 300 block of Harrison was built in 1859. It's named for William Swan, a Union Army veteran, who bought it in 1867. In the 400 block of Harrison is the Robertson Kraft House, a huge Federalist mansion, was built in 1860.

DIRECTIONS:
Turn around here to make your total walking distance about 1.75 miles back to St. Peter Cemetery.

MASONIC LODGE

FIRST ST. PETER CHURCH
SOURCE: KIRKWOOD HISTORICAL SOCIETY

DID YOU KNOW?

St. Peter Catholic Church is Kirkwood's oldest and was established in 1832 on the current site of the cemetery. It's been on the block of Argonne (then Main) between Clay and Harrison since 1867.

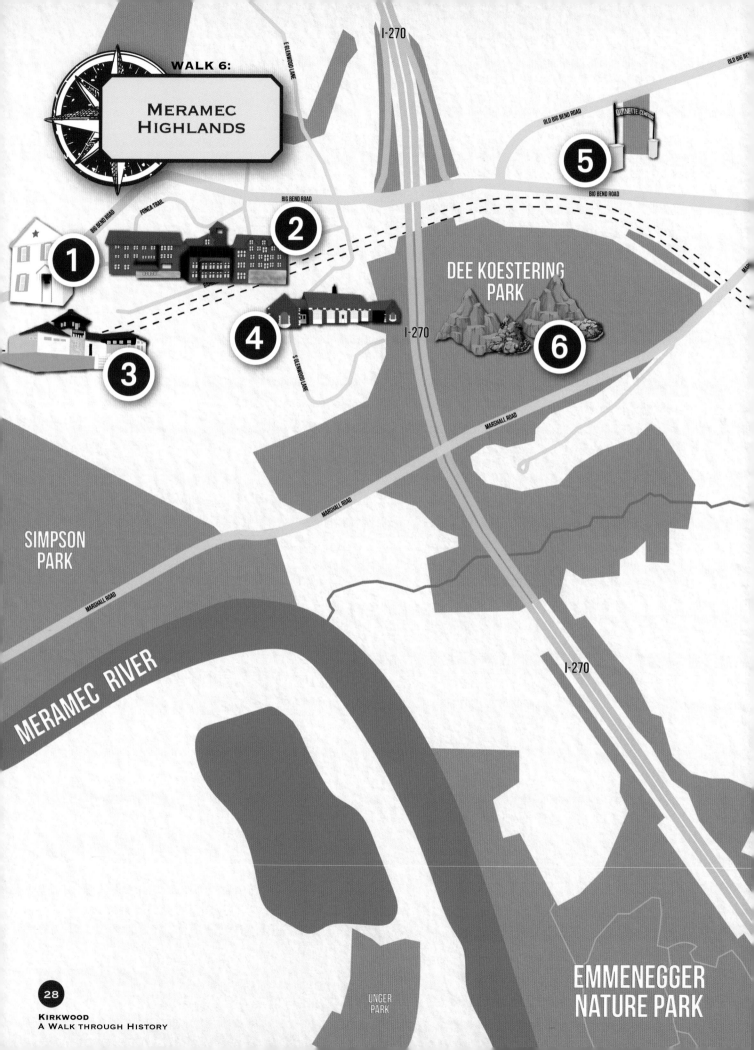

WALK 6:

MERAMEC HIGHLANDS

I-270

E GLENWOOD LANE

OLD BIG BEND

OLD BIG BEND ROAD

QUINETTE CEMETERY

5

OLD BIG BEND ROAD

BIG BEND ROAD

Big Bend Road

BIG BEND ROAD

PONCA TRAIL

2

BIG BEND ROAD

1

BARRETT

DEE KOESTERING
PARK

4

6

S GLENWOOD LANE

I-270

3

MARSHALL ROAD

MARSHALL ROAD

SIMPSON
PARK

MARSHALL ROAD

MERAMEC RIVER

I-270

UNGER
PARK

EMMENEGGER
NATURE PARK

MERAMEC HIGHLANDS

START AND END:
INTERSECTION OF BIG BEND ROAD AND THE WEST END OF PONCA TRAIL
PARKING:
ON PONCA TRAIL (WATCH FOR NO-PARKING SIGNS)
WALKING TOUR DISTANCE:
ABOUT 1.5 MILES FOR SECTION WEST OF I-270; FOUR MILES FOR
THE ENTIRE TOUR.

M**eramec Highlands has a colorful history. At the turn of the 20th century, people from all walks of life came to relax and rejuvenate.** In the 1920s, it was a hotbed of Prohibition-related shenanigans. And in the 1930s it was the site of an epic train crash. Things have calmed considerably since then, but there's still plenty to see in this unique area.

A resort community that opened in 1895, Meramec Highlands included a grand hotel that looked out over the river valley and a beach at what is now Greentree Park.

Marcus Bernheimer modeled the resort after other nearby getaways, such as Sylvan Heights near Kimmswick, which opened in 1880.

Bernheimer created the company to open the resort in 1890, along with a power and water company to bring utilities to the rural area west of Kirkwood. At the time, Kirkwood itself was a dry town, so his decision to get a "dram shop license" from the county caused much clutching of pearls in Kirkwood.

STREETCARS
SOURCE: KIRKWOOD HISTORICAL SOCIETY

 1. GROTH BAR SALOON
PONCA TRAIL AND BIG BEND

At the west end of Ponca Trail and Big Bend Road, the Groth Bar Saloon was the object of much ire and consternation of folks in Kirkwood proper. The building stands across from the former site of the streetcar loop that served the area. Folks hopped off and patronized the saloon, along with the Eden Park Resort just

GROTH BAR SALOON
SOURCE: KIRKWOOD HISTORICAL SOCIETY

to the north. Eden Park was another resort that provided some competition to Meramec but had a vibe more like a carnival than a health spa.

DIRECTIONS:
Walk east on Ponca Trail.

MERAMEC HIGHLANDS HOTEL
SOURCE: KIRKWOOD HISTORICAL SOCIETY

2. HOTEL SITE AND COTTAGES
PONCA TRAIL BETWEEN BIG BEND AND BARBERRY

The centerpiece of the resort was the hotel that looked out over the Meramec River from what is now Ponca Trail, just south of Big Bend Road and up the hill from the railroad tracks. The hotel itself burned down in 1926, and the site

MERAMEC HIGHLANDS COTTAGE

has recently been the target of developers looking to build luxury homes.

For now, the neighborhood is home to most of the original cottages built in the 1890s for visitors to the resort. Many keep their original Victorian charm, with steep roofs, dormers, and diagonal siding. The cottages have names such as Laurel, Elmwood, Ferndale, and Mapleton. They can all be seen during a walk along Ponca Trail.

DIRECTIONS:
Continue on Ponca Trail and then turn right on Barberry Lane. The train station building is on the east side of the street just before it bends at the railroad tracks.

3. FRISCO STATION
1000 BLOCK OF BARBERRY LANE

Much like in downtown Kirkwood and the surrounding areas, the railroad is a key part of this story. In the case of Meramec Highlands, the railroad is the BNSF. Built in 1891, it was the primary mode of transportation for city dwellers looking to reach the nearby resorts. At the height of the resorts' popularity, there were a remarkable nine daily trains each way between St. Louis and Meramec.

FRISCO STATION

From 1930s to 1971, a woman named "Grandma" York lived there and demonstrated making rugs on her loom and spinning wheel to kids from Osage School.

In the early part of the 21st century, the building was rescued from disrepair and turned into a private residence. The owners have kept much of the building's historic detail.

DIRECTIONS:
Return to Big Bend via Barberry and turn right, then turn right on Glenwood Lane.

4. OSAGE HILLS SCHOOL
1110 S. GLENWOOD LANE

The building that now houses Trinity Church on Glenwood Lane was built in 1933 as the local elementary school. When it was first being used as a school, there was no interstate between it and the quarry and local parents wanted the quarry closed because it was an attraction for "undesirables."

OSAGE HILLS SCHOOL
(INSET IMAGE: OSAGE HILLS SCHOOL, CIRCA 1960
SOURCE: THE STATE HISTORICAL SOCIETY OF MISSOURI

Before it was a school, the site and its view of the river were a gathering place for locals where dances and other social events were held.

DIRECTIONS:
To continue the walking tour, retrace your steps on Glenwood Lane, then turn right on Big Bend Road, walk on Big Bend Boulevard; this is a high-traffic area and crosses I-270 on-ramps, so, if you'd rather not walk on Big Bend, return to your vehicle and drive to Quinette Cemetery.

QUINETTE CEMETERY SIGN

5. QUINETTE CEMETERY
CRAIG AT OLD BIG BEND

This was the first burial ground in the St. Louis area and possibly Missouri to be available to Black people. Historians believe it was first used as a cemetery during the Civil War. In 1873, the land was deeded to Olive Chapel A. M. E. Church (see page 26) and became the final resting place of many African-Americans of all backgrounds.

The last burial took place in the 1970s. In 2003, the cemetery was given to the City of Kirkwood as part of a development deal.

At the location, a map on a plaque shows where many of the graves have been detected over the years.

A MEMORIAL TO THOSE,
KNOWN AND UNKNOWN, WHO
SERVED OUR COUNTRY AND
ARE LAID TO REST HERE:

WASHINGTON GREEN, COLORED COOK
7th INFANTRY REGIMENT, COMPANY A
BORN 1818

ARTHUR MASON, PRIVATE 1st CLASS
442nd REGIMENT
1881 - FEB. 26, 1938

WILLIS MITCHELL, PRIVATE
54th REGIMENT,
U.S COLORED INFANTRY, COMPANY C
1847 - 1920

HENRY WHITSON, SERGEANT
65th REGIMENT,
U.S COLORED INFANTRY, COMPANY F
1831 - 1878

GEORGE WASHINGTON WILLIS,
SERGEANT
12th REGIMENT, U.S COLORED

QUINETTE STONE

QUARRY PICNIC AREA
SOURCE: KIRKWOOD HISTORICAL SOCIETY

DIRECTIONS:
Walk on Old Big Bend Road and cross Big Bend Road to continue on Marshall Road.

6. QUARRY AT DEE KOESTERING PARK
1703 MARSHALL ROAD

The quarry at the east end of the Meramec Highlands area was one of the first facilities established by the Meramec Highlands Company. The stone quarried there was used in construction of the hotel and some of the foundations of the cottages.

The Meramec Highlands neighborhood was cut in two when Interstate 270 was built in the 1960s. Some houses were moved due to the freeway right of way to Glenwood Lane. It's made it more difficult for folks to get to the quarry that has been a gathering place for decades. The quarry is now a park that visitors can access via Marshall Road.

VIEW OF TRACKS NEAR SITE OF TRAIN WRECK
SOURCE: KIRKWOOD HISTORICAL SOCIETY

1920s TRAIN WRECK IN MERAMEC HIGHLANDS
SOURCE: KIRKWOOD HISTORICAL SOCIETY

DID YOU KNOW?

When walking across Glenwood Lane, look east toward I-270 to see the site of a great train wreck in 1920. As a result of the wreck, the train tracks were rerouted to lessen the curve.

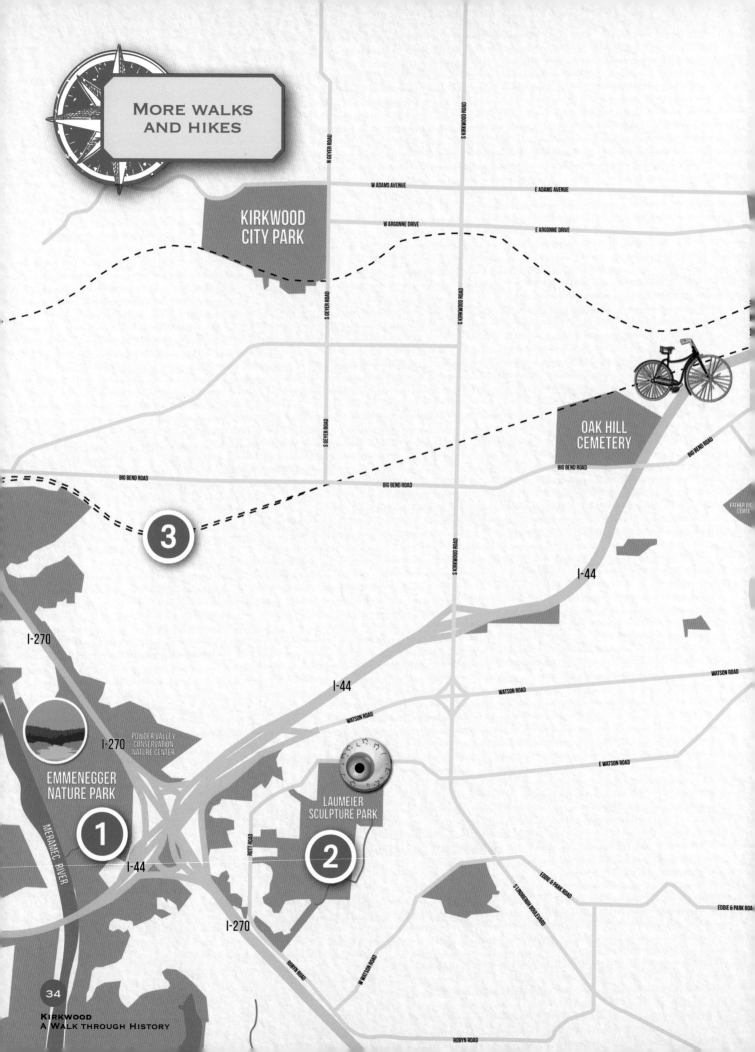

MORE WALKS AND HIKES

KIRKWOOD CITY PARK

N GEYER ROAD

W ADAMS AVENUE

E ADAMS AVENUE

W ARGONNE DRIVE

E ARGONNE DRIVE

S GEYER ROAD

S KIRKWOOD ROAD

OAK HILL CEMETERY

BIG BEND ROAD

BIG BEND ROAD

BIG BEND ROAD

BIG BEND ROAD

FATHER DIC CEME

3

I-270

I-44

S KIRKWOOD ROAD

WATSON ROAD

WATSON ROAD

POWDER VALLEY CONSERVATION NATURE CENTER

I-270

E WATSON ROAD

WATSON ROAD

EMMENEGGER NATURE PARK

LAUMEIER SCULPTURE PARK

1

2

MERAMEC RIVER

I-44

ROTT ROAD

I-270

S LINDBERGH BOULEVARD

EDDIE & PARK ROAD

EDDIE & PARK ROA

ROBYN ROAD

W WATSON ROAD

ROBYN ROAD

MORE WALKS AND HIKES

Kirkwood is blessed to not only have a wealth of urban walks, but many natural areas and off-street trails to explore as well. Lace up your hiking boots and check out these parks and paths.

When walking on a trail in the woods, even if it's a short path, safety comes first. Tell a trusted friend or family member where you are going and when you'll be back. Bring extra water, a hat, and clothes appropriate for the weather. In spring or summer, bring some bug spray to ward off ticks.

1. EMMENEGGER NATURE PARK
STONEYWOOD DRIVE OFF OF I-270

More than 100 acres of woods and hilltop vistas in southwest Kirkwood were once part of the estate of the Lemp family of Lemp Brewery fame. Over the years, the property has been used by the Saint Louis Zoo as a breeding location, and some locals remember when there was a public pool and tennis club.

Today, Emmenegger is a wildly popular hiking spot, where people stroll the paved trails near the Meramec River and hike the challenging dirt paths that reward hikers with views

EMMENEGGER NATURE PARK

across the valley. Its 93 acres were once owned by a real estate developer named Russell Emmenegger, who donated the property to Kirkwood. The city and the Missouri Conservation Department jointly operate the area, along with the adjacent 15-acre Possum Woods Conservation Area.

Near the parking lot, Emmenegger has picnic shelters and about a third of a mile of paved trail accessible to wheelchairs and strollers. There are lots of spots to view the Meramec River.

LEMP ESTATE
SOURCE: KIRKWOOD HISTORICAL SOCIETY

Hikers can head slightly uphill to the north and take the one-mile dirt trail along a lovely creek nestled in woods, which include oaks and other native trees. After about half a mile, the trail turns to the west and goes steeply uphill. After this short climb, the trail turns south, and hikers will get views across the Meramec Valley as they hike along the ridge.

In the spring and fall, watch for volunteers pulling invasive honeysuckle shrubs from the forest floor. These invasive bushes leaf out before native species, sucking up nutrients and blocking out the sun before desirable plants can get a foothold. These invaders have run rampant over Missouri in recent decades, but volunteers and conservation department officials have been slowly gaining ground in the honeysuckle war.

Directions to Emmenegger: From Geyer Road in Kirkwood, just north of I-44, go west on Cragwold Road. Drive around Powder Valley Nature Center and veer left to cross I-270, then turn left on Stoneywood Drive. The road ends at the Emmenegger parking area.

2. LAUMEIER SCULPTURE PARK
12580 ROTT ROAD

Just south of the Kirkwood city limits is one of the true gems of St. Louis County—a world-class outdoor sculpture park. Perhaps most famous for its giant eyeball, this park covers more than 100 acres with dozens of larger-than-life sculptures. Some encourage visitors to climb in

LAUMEIER SCULPTURE PARK

and around. One section even welcomes dogs to explore exhibits specially made for them. Cromlech Glen is perhaps the largest sculpture in the park at almost a half acre. It resembles the nest of a giant mythical creature and visitors are invited to walk the elevated earthen perimeter and down into the bowl.

Admission to the sculpture park is free (aside from some special weekend events) and trails crisscross the forests and fields. A paved trail that's about two-thirds of a mile shows off many of the park's best-known works. There's an "art hike" through the woods that's about three-quarters of a mile and other side trails that can provide hours of pleasant strolling.

GENERAL GRANT'S LOG CABIN
SOURCE: LIBRARY OF CONGRESS

3. GRANT'S TRAIL
KIRKWOOD TRAILHEAD IS AT LEFFINGWELL AND HOLMES

One of the best-known attractions in Missouri is the Katy Trail, a 240-mile-long dedicated bike path through the heart of the state. Another rails-to-trails success story begins in Kirkwood. Grant's Trail welcomes about half a million visitors a year on the former bed of the Kirkwood-Carondelet Branch of the Pacific Railroad that rolls past; at Kirkwood's famous train station. The last engines rolled off this line in 1990, and local trail and parks boosters

moved quickly to acquire the land. In the decades since, the trail has continued to expand, and Kirkwood hopes to acquire the land to get it to reach all the way downtown. Grant's Trail ends near Big Bend Blvd. and I-44 about a mile from the train station.

A main attraction on the trail is Grant's Farm and Grant Historic Site. Grant's Farm is part animal park and part beer garden. Entrance is free, but there's a charge for parking, so if you pedal or walk from another location on Grant's Trail, you save the fee.

Ulysses S. Grant National Historic Site, just across the trail from Grant's Farm, features a visitor center and museum dedicated to the 18th president. The property was home to Grant's wife, Julia's, family, when they met while Grant was stationed at Jefferson Barracks about five miles south, in 1844. The couple later lived on the property themselves.

Local cycling enthusiasts use Grant's Trail to connect to other off-road paths. Some road riding between trails is often necessary, but cyclists can ride dozens of miles on Grant's Trail and River Des Peres Greenway.

GRANT'S FARM

ACKNOWLEDGMENTS

This book would not have been possible without the hard work and dedication of the Kirkwood Historical Society volunteers at Mudd's Grove. John Crowley spent many hours with me in the Gould Library as I scanned texts and photos and looked through the binders and books full of meticulously curated information.

James Baker was the source for much of the information about Meramec Highlands. He's written multiple books on the subject and lives in the house that was the general store serving the Highlands.

My thanks as well to Harriet Patton for introducing me to so many people and their memories of Meacham Park; Ted Wight for a tour of the Bohemian Enclave; Jim Vatterott, Joy Weese Moll, Sherry Bonham, and Christie Lee.

Josh Stevens, Amanda Doyle, Barbara Northcott, Lori Newhouse, and all the crew at Reedy Press deserve my thanks for their support in every step of the process of the creation of this book.

FURTHER READING

The following books are available at Mudd's Grove for purchase or viewing, or via local library systems:

Discovering African American St. Louis, John A. Wright

Glimpses of Meramec Highlands, James F. Baker

Gone but not Forgotten: Quinette Cemetery, A Slave Burial Ground, est. 1866, Keith Rawlings

A History of Kirkwood, Missouri 1851-1965, June Wilkinson Dahl

A Brief History of Meacham Park, Missouri, Lonnie R. Speer

On the web:

Grace Episcopal Church has extensive history, baptism, marriage, and burial records on its website at gracekirkwood.org.

The City of Kirkwood's Historic Preservation website has maps of each historic district with parcel-level detail, a listing of each local landmark, and a listing of all properties on the National Register of Historic Places.

The Kirkwood Historical Society's Mudd's Grove houses a museum and extensive library of magazines, books, newspaper clippings, and primary sources. Contact them via kirkwoodhistoricalsociety.com to make an appointment.

INDEX